All Penelope Phillips wanted was closure; a chance to say goodbye to her father. One final conversation with the man who held her world together with a simple timeless melody.

It has been ten years since his passing and Penelope has found his last location after a fight with her mother. She leaves with nothing more than a scribbled note and the courage to drive into the unknown, looking for a hero.

Her journey will take her farther than she could have ever imagined as she searches for answers only fate can provide.

Penny Lane

By Rick Kaiser

"This is a must read!!! My first book since finishing school...just beautiful. Thanks **Rick Kaiser**! You rocked this one"

"Fantastic!!"

"I loved it"

"Couldn't put it down"

"This is the most beautiful story I have ever read"

"He is so talented"

"I bawled my eyes out"

"Brilliantly written and touches your emotions deeply from page to page. Wow!"

"Loved your book! I might be a blubbering mess right now."

"Penny Lane is a precious book; once I started reading, I could not put it down!"

Book #1 of 4

Penny Lane

Peggy Sue

Bobby & Penny

Bud & Annie

"It is here that I am home

Under the leaves of the Meraki tree

I drink with the Logophilia

Sipping words from cloudy tea

I bury my toes in the warming sand

And feel its grit between my teeth

As I strain to hold this fragile oasis

In the midst of troubled seas"

Rick Kaiser

Penny Lane

By Rick Kaiser

Preface

I really don't know where to begin.
Writing a book seems easy enough; I've read
hundreds of them and colored outside the lines
in just as many, so why the struggle? Maybe I
could start on the last page with "The End" and
work my way backwards? I am sitting at a rustic
kitchen table on a rainy day, attempting to pen
the great American novel and possibly garner a
few paychecks along the way. The day-to-day
drivel I write is fairly easy and the occasional
short story has been the deepest venture I have
attempted. To sit down and fabricate
characters, develop their history, paint their

personality and breathe life into them seems as difficult as shaving an angry wolverine with a butter knife. I have hundreds of personas and chapters floating on my inky sea of discourse, yet the minute I sit and place pen to paper, I freeze. Pat Conroy said, "Fantasy is the souls' brightest porcelain" and I have read every one of his porcelain treasures. He thrust himself into each of his characters for just a short period of time, rewriting history until the last page bid his fantasy adieu. There are hundreds of things I wish I could change about yesterday, but I cannot. I have imagined details that never existed and outcomes that only happen in Hollywood and if I close my laptop and walk away from this table right now, Penelope Phillips will never begin her journey from a small farm town in central Illinois, in a beige station wagon, looking for her father.

Chapter 1

She made it as far as the Mississippi before the radiator in the wagon sent up a geyser of steam and forced her into a Walmart parking lot just outside of Quincy. The nametag on the tow truck driver's greasy shirt read, "Bud". He had kind eyes, as though he had been meant for greater things but greater things got in the way. Penelope thanked him, climbed into the passenger seat and was greeted by the scent of oil and grease. She thought of her grandfather and the short summer she spent at the farm helping Grandma take lunch out to the boys. It was her only memory of him, one she kept close. The truck bounced and slowed down as they pulled into a ramshackle garage, complete with half a dozen cars on the lot and a wall of used tires stacked against the side. Bud opened the shop door and waved toward an old dusty davenport, complete with antiquated magazines; "You can wait over here Miss", he said kindly. She walked over, moved a few magazines and sat down.

Bud worked on the car for quite some time, yet Penelope waited patiently. She picked up a few magazines out of boredom, pretended to read and sat them down slowly as to not offend Bud. She thought it was funny she would be concerned for this old mechanic, but something about him intrigued her. His eyes were a deep grey that seemed to hold back a river of tears or a thousand smiles, she couldn't figure out which.

"Pit Stop!" Her mother yelled. She hated that name and vowed to change it as soon as she was able. "PITSTOP!" she yelled again. "What do you want" Penelope screamed back. "Come here when I call you!" Her mother demanded. She rose from her bed and walked toward the kitchen where she would find the loathsome creature, washing down Xanax with a box of wine. "Will you run to the store for mama? I'm out of cigarettes."
"No Mom, I'm busy."
"With what!?" she snapped. "You hide in that damn room all the time reading your stupid

books! You're young, you should be out having the time of your life chasing boys!"

"And look where it got you!" Penelope snapped back.

That was enough. Her mother looked at her through dead eyes, as though she were the abomination that destroyed such a promising life. Penelope grabbed the wad of money and her coat, knowing this battle would never end until one of them was dead.

"Don't forget my cigarettes" her mother shouted as Penelope slammed the back door.

"Miss" "MISS!" Bud was standing over the couch with a tender look. "I'm sorry ma'am, but I'm not going to be able to repair the car properly until tomorrow morning. The part I need is just a few blocks from here, but they're closed for the day. Do you have a place to stay?"

She gathered her wits quickly and said no. "Is there a hotel within walking distance?" she asked.

"Yes, there is but I could give you a ride to a nicer one. It's just a few miles and I certainly don't mind. As a matter of fact, I would feel better if you let me drive you."

"Ok, thank you." She said automatically.

"Are you ok Miss?" Bud asked the question slowly, with a genuine concern.

"Yes. Yes, I'm okay. It's just been a long day and I wasn't expecting car troubles."

"If you don't mind me askin, where you headin?" Bud twanged just a little to lighten her mood.

Before she could pose an answer the words just tumbled out; "I don't know."

Bud sat quietly for a moment and then began to speak very softly as if he had not heard her.

"My wife Annie is in a wheelchair but that has never slowed her down in the kitchen. She's probably there right now, putting the finishing touches on a roast that Jesus would show up for. I have a feeling she would like to meet you Miss. Why don't you come and have some dinner with us?"

Penelope felt a little uncomfortable. She seldom trusted anyone thanks to the ghoul that posed as her mother. Every friend she had ever brought home felt the acid tongue of contempt, and they seldom returned.

"Sir, that's ok. I don't want to intrude. I'll be fine at the hotel."

Bud insisted and Penelope didn't put up much of a fight. She didn't want to be alone in a strange town anyway.

"You'll be just fine Miss Penelope." It was the first time he had called her by her name and she liked the way it sounded coming from him. Bud turned the radio on.

Chapter 2

♫ Penny Lane is in my head and in my eyes, there beneath the blue suburban skies......♪ [1]

"Penny Lane! Penny Lane!" Her dad was the only one who called her that. He always came into the house singing that old Beatles song and she would stop what she was doing and run toward his voice. "Daddy!" she squealed with delight as she leapt into his arms. He would twirl her around as he continued singing. "How's my sweet Penny Lane?" he sang. "Daddy I missed you! How long are you staying?" she always asked and he always replied; "As long as there's a smile, I'll stay another mile." She clenched her teeth together and smiled so big she felt like the corners of her mouth would meet in the back of her tiny head. "Aahhh, that's my girl, looks like I'm going to be here awhile." He gave her a zerbert on her cheek and she squealed with laughter.

Bud clicked off the radio and turned into the driveway of a modest brick ranch. He shut off the motor and halfheartedly said; "This is it." Penelope wondered for a moment what the heck she was doing voluntarily going to a stranger's house? A wave of trepidation swept over her as she wished she would have gone to a motel, yet the feeling passed quickly. There was nothing malicious about this tender giant that frightened her, and she couldn't imagine him hurting a cricket. She got out and followed him up the ramp to the front door. He opened the door and stepped inside, holding the door for her as he bellowed toward the other room; "Annie, I'm home and we've got some company." He turned his head and smiled for the first time, "I hope you're hungry", he said with a grin.

A wispy, mellifluous voice sang from the other side of the house, "Bud?"

"Yes honey, I'm home. Come meet Penelope." Annie rolled into the room in her chair. She was strikingly beautiful; frail but elegant with alabaster skin and the bluest eyes Penelope had ever seen. She rolled to Penelope without saying a word, stopped and leaned forward taking her hand in hers. Her eyes never left Penelope's face as she squeezed her hands ever so lightly and smiled.

"Welcome friend," she said in the most exquisite tone Penelope had ever heard. It was if Heaven had just greeted her and she was momentarily overwhelmed by the grace this woman exuded. All she could manage was a squeaky, "Hi."

"Bud are you going to introduce me to our guest?" she asked while holding her gaze.

"Oh, I'm sorry. Honey this is Penelope and her car broke down and I didn't have the part in stock so I had to order it and it won't be in till tomorrow morning, so I was going to take her to a…   "

"It is a pleasure to meet you Penelope. Welcome to our home." Annie said, gently cutting off Bud's nervous rambling.

Penelope giggled as this regal woman continued to hold her in her gaze.

"Please come in sweetheart and make yourself at home." Annie gracefully spun the chair and moved into the family room. Bud made his way down the hall to change clothes as Penelope followed Annie. The house was warm and lived in; Annie managed to keep a whole lot of everything in place without running out of places. Picture frames dotted the walls, end tables and fireplace mantle with dozens of smiling faces frozen in time. The large frame in the center of the mantle caught her attention. It was a picture of a little girl, possibly 10 years old, holding a stuffed bear. She looked a lot like Annie, the same alabaster skin and eyes that disarmed and drew you in. "It must be their daughter", she thought.

"Penelope are you hungry?"

"Ma'am, I appreciate your hospitality so much, you really don't have to feed me."

Penelope lied; she was starving.

"Nonsense my friend. Bud is already setting a place for you." Her insistence was more of a prayer than a demand and Penelope knew she could not say no. "Follow me into the dining room?"

"Yes ma'am." Penelope felt like she was in a dream, this morning seemed like a lifetime ago. She felt as if she might burst into tears at any moment and she didn't know why. She steeled herself, took a breath and followed Annie into the dining room.

The table was small but accommodating; four chairs with more than a few meals under them, but it was cozy. There were three settings complete with linen napkins. A vase of fresh flowers competed with a tantalizing roast as the aromas mingled together and danced upon her senses. Bud pulled her chair out for her and quickly moved to the other side to push Annie's chair closer to the table. Penelope admired him; his love and devotion toward her was so palpable. She let a smile touch the corner of her mouth.

"Where's your mama Penny Lane?" Her father asked in that sing song voice of his.

"She went to the store to get something for dinner."

"She did? I was going to take you both to dinner." He grabbed her by the hand and pretended to be a prince escorting her to the ball. "This way my love, magic awaits tonight at the prestigious Castle of Cheese, home of Lord Chuck E., Purveyor of all things gooey!"

Penelope let out a cheer; "Yes my prince, let all our kingdom dine on pepperoni this magic eve!"

She had played this little game with him as far back as she could remember and adored his imagination.

The back door slammed and her mother yelled from the kitchen. "Dinner is served! If you want to eat, it's on the counter." Her dad put his finger to his lips as if to shush her disappointment and whispered, "Tonight, we will dine on wildebeest and the spoils of conquest, come my queen!" He put her on his shoulders and carried her into the kitchen. A few fast food bags rested on the counter and he scooped them up and carried her and the food to the table. He tore into his food and pretended to be a barbarian; "Where's my whiskey!?" he cried. Penelope poured a glass of tea for him and said in her best scullery maid voice, "Keep ya shirt on lug, it's rut here." They both burst out laughing. Her mother yelled from behind the closed bedroom door, "Don't you make a mess in there!" Penelope rolled her eyes theatrically and wondered why she always said that? Her mother never cleaned the kitchen, she did.

"Penelope. Penelope." Annie reached out and touched her hand, "Would you like some potatoes?" "Yes, yes ma'am." Penelope stammered. "I'm sorry, I've had a lot on my mind. Today has been kind of a blur." "That's ok sweetheart." Annie said in that perfect tone, "We're all entitled to more than a few. You can relax now. Bud will have you all fixed up in the morning and you can be on your way." Penelope thanked her.
"If you don't mind me asking my dear, where are you going?" Annie inquired. Penelope

paused momentarily yet the moment felt like eternity. Less than a day ago she had slammed the back door and pointed the car west. "I'm going to visit an old friend." She replied. "I need some advice."

"Good advice is a priceless treasure, Miss Penelope." Bud chimed in, "My Annie is always giving me an earful of it and I certainly need it." He smiled at Annie and reached out to touch her hand, she met him halfway. Penelope watched this couple and envied their genuine love for one another. They glanced up at her and she smiled for the first time and before she knew it the words just came tumbling out; "You guys are beautiful." Her face flushed with embarrassment as she looked down at her plate. Bud reacted quickly and said; "Well I've been called a whole lotta things in my life but beautiful ain't never been one of them. Thank you, sweetie, I think you just made my day." He raised his glass of tea and proclaimed a toast; "To Bud the beautiful!" Annie giggled as they all lifted their glasses and toasted Bud. Penelope thought of her father.

Chapter 3

Jack Phillips was tired. He had spent the last six days navigating the arteries of the Midwest, hawking the latest and greatest mouse trap. That's what he told people when asked of his profession; he was a salesman. It didn't matter what he sold just as long as he sold it. He had good months but never great, and bad months that outweighed every good one he ever had. Still, he peddled from town to town, knocking on doors and spinning tall tales of wonderous gadgets and widgets that could and would, save you millions. This was never a dream, just a necessity he had long ago resigned himself to. It paid his bills and kept Penny Lane full and warm, and that was enough. She was a beautiful accident that became the best thing that ever happened to him. He smiled to himself over his second cup of coffee at a truck stop outside of Columbia. He remembered the day she was born; he had driven through the night with the radio blasting and got there just in the nick of time. Penelope Lane Phillips had come into the world at 1:13 am and he wept openly. He slept on the couch at the hospital for two days and waited to take his precious little Penny Lane home.

She made things tenable for a little while, he and Penny's mother never saw eye to eye on anything. Her own failures and countless relations prior, had thickened her skin and chaffed any tenderness left imbued in an already broken heart. But Jack tried, only to watch her from across the room as she sat on the edge of the bed wringing her hands, as darkness gathered like storm clouds on the periphery of her anguish. The soft edge of her frayed innocence did little to comfort the sorrow that paced behind her wilted dark eyes. She would stare into the abyss like a lover; a flickering lamppost on a shadowy corner and he, a sunrise that would never come.

Jack did all he could, helping her through a monstrous wall of postpartum depression that scared the hell out of him. He was never sure they would be there when he returned from the

*road and sure enough, he came home one day
to an empty house and a wilted rose on the keys
of an old piano that never played a sadder song.*

*The sun pierced the blinds that day and bled
through the grey, as dust particles hung
indolently in the gold strands that sliced the
shadows.*
She was a melody he could not sing.
*A neon ribbon against a chrome sky only canvas
could hear. And he, a book she had no interest
in reading;*
another story of a fool and a wishing well.
*Saying goodbye was too pedestrian for her, too
gauche.*
*She preferred an empty train station on a rainy
day, a haunting farewell that would linger long
after her train wreck was gone.*
*He finished his coffee, walked out into a
downpour and never saw her again.*

Chapter 4

Penny insisted she take care of the dinner table and the dishes for Annie; it was the least she could do. She gathered the dishes as Annie gracefully maneuvered around her, pointing out the dish soap and the garbage can. "The Tupperware is in the bottom cabinet dear; I keep everything low, for obvious reasons." Annie smiled and pleaded in her sing song voice, "Please let me help." Penny finally acquiesced and the two of them made short work of dinner.

Penny was wiping her hands and noticed another picture of the young girl she saw on the mantelpiece. "Annie is this your daughter?" She inquired innocently. Annie paused momentarily as a dark shadow briefly touched her face. "Yes" she said tenderly. "She was our little Abigail." "Was?" Penny asked as if she were tip toeing. The air seemed to leave the room as the fumes from a lighthearted dinner dissipated in the anguish that threatened to choke Annie's voice.

She leaned back ever so slightly, making sure Bud was out of earshot and answered.

"I met Bud in high school. He was a gentle giant with the heart of a child. He worked at his dad's garage every day after school and seldom had time for activities, until I stopped one day to see if he could fix my car." Annie glanced in the living room again, speaking in almost a whisper. "He fixed it for free and asked if he could take me out for a burger. I said it was probably not a good idea and it was his reply that has never left me. He simply said; 'Annie I had to ask, all I have are my words and you are the most beautiful girl I have ever seen. I certainly apologize if I made you uncomfortable. Please forgive me'." Annie momentarily drifted off on the wings of a distant memory and Penny let her go.

"We have been together ever since," she said.

Annie began to walk through her life as the words she spoke leapt from her lips on gossamer wings. Penny listened intently as Annie spoke of proms and holidays and weddings and joy. Annie took a breath, looked into the living room where Bud had fallen asleep watching TV and took a dark turn toward the pain that hid behind her resolve.

"Abigail was ten years old. We were coming home from a long weekend away. It was late in the evening, in a downpour. It was so difficult to see. I asked Bud if he was ok to drive and he said, 'Of course'. He tried to merge onto the highway...but a semi cut us off," Annie's voice began to crack. "Bud slammed on the brakes and cut the wheel to avoid going off the embankment." She was breathing heavily now. "He swerved just behind the truck but there was another car directly behind him. We hit that car...so hard. I can still hear the metal grinding and tearing.
Somehow, we became locked up and went tumbling down the embankment. I don't remember anything after that. I woke in the hospital a few days later with one very broken

man standing over me. I lost more than my legs that day Penny, I lost my daughter and my husband has never been able to forgive himself." She stopped speaking for a moment as one lone tear made its way down her alabaster cheek. "We have never been the same Penny. The loss of a child is a sorrow that can never be satiated. It is a bloodless wound that will not scar; it opens every holiday, every birthday and every time someone like you, walks into Bud's garage. He cannot forgive himself. He relives the moment over and over and over, wishing he could go back, and not start that car."

Annie paused, took a deep breath and managed a thin smile toward Penny.
Penny walked over to her chair, her own heart broken for these beautiful strangers and asked if she could give her a hug.

"Of course you can, sweetheart." Penny leaned down, put her arms around her neck and they both began to cry.

Penny woke to the sound of someone clanking around the house. For a moment she forgot where she was and had to do a slow inventory to make sure she hadn't gone crazy. She got up slowly, went into the tiny bathroom next to her room and splashed cold water on her face. She heard the tow truck rumble to life and back out of the driveway. She followed the hallway into the front room in time to see Bud pull away. Annie was in the kitchen pouring a cup of coffee,

"Good morning Penelope, I hope you slept well. Would you like cream and sugar?" Annie was unflappable. They had held each other for several minutes last night and this morning she was a picture of grace and kindness.

"Thank you, Annie, yes cream and sugar please and thank you. I hope I didn't overstep my bounds last night; Are you ok? Where did Bud go?" She said in one breath and realized she gave no room for an answer.

"I'm sorry, just feeling a little awkward."

"Penny, there is no need to feel that way, how were you to know? Besides, each time I talk about it I find a little bit more peace and I need to find a little more, every day, so...thank you." Annie assured her. "And Bud went to pick up the part for your car, he said you needed a dump?"

"No, good grief, that's not it. A pump, your car needs a pump." Annie started giggling and they both burst out laughing. Penny could not stop laughing as she imagined that old station wagon squatting on a toilet, straining its headlights and grimacing. They both had tears in their eyes as the uproar simmered down and Annie caught her off guard:

"What are you running from Penny?"

Penny stared at the floor, in spite of her discomfort she felt safe. She knew Annie cared. So, she began.

"When I left the house yesterday, I thought I was running from her, my mother. Her name is Peggy Sue, seriously, after the Buddy Holly song." Penny said sarcastically. "I have hated her for so long I cannot remember if I ever loved her. When my dad was alive it was a little different, he would come and rescue me, faithfully, every other weekend. I would wait from one weekend to the next for him to come. He always had Penny Lane playing on his car stereo when he pulled in the driveway..."

Penny smiled, with tears in her eyes as the glue from that moment, painted an everlasting souvenir that covered an entire wall in her memory, and Annie let her stay there as long as she needed.

"My mom acted like she hated him but I know she didn't. My dad was a beautiful dreamer and my mom is, well, a hard realist driven by a vicious taskmaster; failure. She makes herself strong only to fall apart on those closest to her, which just happens to be me. She grew up in a loveless environment, void of men. Her mother was exactly the same and if it wasn't for my dad, I would probably be the same. He rescued me. I wanted to be just like him, I loved his laugh, his sense of humor, his creativity and most of all, his sincerity. He loved me and I don't think there was anything he wouldn't have done for me. When I lost him, I lost the only thing I looked forward to. My mom locked herself in her bedroom for days because she couldn't stand to hear me cry over him. 'Her words'." Penny quoted. "It has been ten years since he left and not until last night, did I have any hope at all of moving forward, starting over. A chance to hold him in my memory without cutting myself to pieces on the jagged edges of unbearable sorrow," She paused and looked up at Annie, "and then I met you."

"We have so much in common and somehow, some weird way I ended up in your kitchen last night. I have known you for less than 24 hours and I feel safer with you than I have ever felt with my own mother. We both have experienced incredible loss yet you radiate a grace that I cannot fathom. I know this probably sounds really stupid but I needed to meet you and if there is a God in Heaven then I am convinced He arranged it because I shouldn't be here. But here I am. Annie, please tell me it's going to be ok!" Penelope was crying now. "You don't even have to mean it; I just want to hear YOU say it. Just one time Annie, please, before I go." Penelope was sobbing now. All the years of angst, sorrow and blight ran down her face in a torrent of surrender. Annie rolled to her, grabbed her head in her hands and held her like she was her own. She let her cry as the sobs wracked her body. As her tears subsided, Annie placed her lips near Penelope's ear and whispered, "it's going to be ok Penny Lane." Penelope burst into tears again.

Bud pulled into the drive a few hours later and came in with news that Miss Penelope's mighty stallion was road worthy and ready for adventure.

Penelope stood and let out an audible sigh. Her eyes were swollen from crying so hard and Bud asked if she was ok. Penny smiled and said, "Of course, I didn't sleep very well but thank you for asking Bud." She was genuinely sincere and a little sad that she was leaving these wonderful strangers who had opened their home and their hearts to her. She looked around the room slowly and her eyes came to rest on Annie. Annie's eyes met hers and she smiled with that warm disarming grace that first caught Penny's attention. "Thank you so much," Penny said. "I don't believe I will ever forget you." Before Annie could say a word, Bud whipped out a fresh business card with three different phones numbers scrawled on the back and began to tell Penelope how she could reach them if she ever needed anything, with the emphasis on ANYTHING!

"Miss Penelope, you don't owe me a thing for the car. It was a pleasure having you stay with us and you sure brightened our day and I know I can speak for my Annie when I say she really loved...." Annie gently and tactfully interrupted her stammering husband, "Penelope, it was more than a pleasure meeting you and I have a feeling we will see each other again. You are always welcome."

Penelope leaned over and hugged Annie tight, she stood up, walked across the room and threw her arms around Bud and laid her head on his chest. "Thank you, Mr. Bud." She said like a child. Bud choked up a little as he wrapped his arms around Penelope and did his best to maintain his composure. "You be careful Miss Penelope. If you have any trouble with your car you be sure to call me and I'll come running anytime, day or night. Alright?"

"Yessir Mr. Bud" Penny replied with a smile. Bud walked her out to the driveway where her old station wagon idled smoothly.
Annie waited on the porch as Bud doted over Penelope, held the door for her and closed it gently. She backed out slowly, took one long look, tapped her horn and drove away

Chapter 5

Peggy Sue turned the pages of an old photo album slowly, reminiscing and reliving every moment of her tragic youth. She had blossomed in the middle of her sophomore year and made the boys who had called her "Fatty Frosh", eat her pain. She lost her baby fat and was strikingly beautiful, never afraid to speak her mind. Her father left when she was 8 years old, worn out from a marriage that began circling the drain while the vows still hung in the air.

Peggy Sue lived under the toxic umbrella of her mother's angst and before long the acrid barbs of hatred pierced her tender juvenescence and poisoned the bloodstream of her youth. She loved the attention she got from the boys in town, but she loved the men more. Business owners, a few teachers and even a wayward preacher fell under the spell of the storm called Peggy Sue. She hung around the small farm town for a few years after high school and as her popularity waned, she decided it was time to make something of herself. She packed a few belongings, drained her mother's bank account and headed north in hopes of finding something more than a slow death in a little town. She made it to the western suburbs of Chicago, found a small apartment and within days had a job at a car dealership as a receptionist. She was a nice addition to the company, especially among the salesmen and eventually her promiscuity landed her in the unemployment line. She spent two weeks in bed, struggling with the depression that would eventually own her soul. She got up, dressed and went to the local community college.

Peggy Sue was going to be somebody.

She turned the page of her photo album and landed on a picture of Jack. He was young then; she had met him over a cup of coffee soon after her first classes had started. She stopped at a little coffee shop between class and he was sitting in the front of the shop, with a small speaker and a very beat up guitar. He looked up at her, smiled and began to sing an old Buddy

*Holly song that caused her knees to buckle. Her
face flushed and the Peggy Sue that was always
in control, lost control and had to sit down.*

*She let a smile touch the corners of her lips as
she traced her finger across his picture; he was
her favorite mistake and she had certainly made
a lot of them. She remembered the late nights,
sitting in the front row as he chased a dream
that she knew would fail. Jack was fun so she
hung around and loved the attention she got
from being his arm candy. She followed him to
Madison one weekend for a big show he was
doing with a local headliner, he was so excited.
She drank too much that weekend and several
weeks later, the hangover came in the form of a
positive pregnancy test. She was a fool! How
could she get knocked up by some guitar toting
hopeless stargazer? When she confronted him
and asked him to pay for the abortion, he
stammered. "You're what?? How? I mean I
know how but I thought you said you were..."
He stopped and simply said, "I want you to have*

the baby. That, I will help you do and if you're so inclined, I will help you raise our child."

Peggy turned the page again; pictures of birthday cake, holidays, first school days and balloons filled the leaves as she continued to turn. She landed on the picture of a highway mile marker; it was the closest thing she had to a headstone. She covered the picture with her hand and convinced herself sometimes fate knows what's best, she didn't have to compete with him anymore.

She lifted her hand and noticed the empty space next to the photo. The small handwritten note from the sheriff's department, was gone. She sat straight up and knew where Pitstop was going.

Penny pulled over in a gas station just south of Hickory Grove. Bud had made sure her gas gauge was pointed as far right as it would go, so gas was not what she needed.

She opened her purse, retrieved her wallet, and took out the small piece of notebook paper she had found in her mother's photo album. Penny had stumbled upon the book a few days ago while her mother was out with God knows who, and spent the entire evening memorizing every picture. Her dad and mom holding her when she was a tiny infant. Her dad kissing her mother on the cheek as she crinkled up her nose and smiled. It was a time Penny had so little memory of that it seemed like a Hallmark movie that happened to other people, never her.

She found the picture of the mile marker and the small piece of paper that she now held; the last place her father was alive and the only headstone this bizarre world had provided her. She would finally have a chance to lay flowers upon the side of a forgotten road near the state line and mourn. She headed south on 172 and as she neared East Hannibal, she started looking for the Payson Road exit. She saw the exit and turned her blinker on; she eased onto the offramp, followed it around to a two-way stop and sat there; a low hum reverberated in her ears as the blood flowed from her thundering heart. The traffic seemed to slow and disappear as she stared at a fresh white cross, on the other side of the culvert.

Chapter 6

Bud was in a very dark place. His head thundered as he imagined a cool drenching torrent of rain soothing the pounding in his head. He wanted to sleep but a foreboding shadow crept along the edge of this bizarre dream as thunder clouds roiled along the edge of his lucidity and began to whisper his name; "wake up Bud. Wake Up Bud. WAKE UP BUD!!" The voice yanked him from his concussion as rain poured in where the windows used to be; he sat motionless for a moment, trying to get his bearings. A wave of nausea swept over him suddenly and he vomited all over his shirt and wondered why he felt so bad. A jolt of searing pain shot up his shoulder as he raised his arm to wipe his mouth. The realization came slowly at first then shocked him into coherency. They had crashed.

"Annie! Abigail!"

Terror struck with breathtaking ferocity as he immediately forgot his pain and tore himself loose from the seatbelt. His leg was twisted beneath the dash but he never felt it. Herculean strength surged through his body as adrenaline pumped into every muscle and he tore himself from the wreckage. He never felt the crushed discs in his back nor the break in his ankle. The rain washed the blood from his eyes and the gash in his scalp; he would never remember the pain. He ripped the door from its hinges and pulled his unconscious wife from the front seat, carrying her like a baby just a few feet away. He dove into the back seat and gently lifted the lifeless body of his daughter Abigail and laid her next to her mother.
Bud was in shock.

"Annie? Abigail?" it was more of a question than a cry, choking back tears. "Annie and Abigail", he spoke again, his voice rising. "ANNIE and ABIGAIL!", this time he howled above the sound of the approaching siren. Bud was outside of his mind when the officer knelt

beside him. The EMT arrived shortly after and
they were forced to subdue him with a sedative
before they could treat his girls. Bud slipped into
a troubled dark sleep, filled with twisted metal
and the sound of rain.

Penelope sat by the side of the road with the
engine running, wondering who would place
flowers at her father's crash site? "Who put the
cross here?" "Am I in the right place?" "Did
mom come all this way?" A dozen questions
careened off the walls of her vulnerable
rationale like an angry pinball. She turned the
motor off and stared at the steering wheel. She
took several deep breaths and placed her hand
on the door handle. Curiosity finally got the
best of her and she opened the door, stepped
out of the car and stared at the little white
cross. There were several old flowers around it
and what looked like a picture. Surely, she must
be in the wrong place. She put one foot in front
of the other and began to move forward, she
did not look up until she was right on top of the

cross. She knelt down with her eyes closed, placed her hand on the small crossbeam and opened her eyes.

Chapter 7

Peggy Sue sat on the front porch smoking a cigarette, staring off into nothing. Penelope saw her as she weaved her Schwinn bicycle down the street, between the yellow lines. She quickly jumped the curb onto the sidewalk before her mother could see her. Her mother never turned her head. Penelope was momentarily relieved until she realized she had never seen this look before. Something was wrong.

She rode up to the porch, put her kickstand down and looked at her mother. "Mama?" Peggy Sue never flinched. "Mama what's wrong?" Penelope was worried. Peggy Sue took a deep drag on her cigarette, blew the smoke out slowly and looked at Penelope. "How's my Penny Lane?" Penelope was startled. Her mother never called her that. "Mama what's wrong?" Penelope asked. Peggy Sue's empty smile barely contained the horror that lie behind her hollow sentiment

Penelope screamed this time; "MAMA!!! WHATS WRONG!?!"

Peggy Sue answered in a toneless staccato, void of hope: "Penny your father will not be picking you up this weekend." She paused for effect, "As a matter of fact, your father will not be picking you up anymore. I'm sorry Penny Lane, your father is gone." Penelope stood shaking her head in disbelief. "What are you talking about mama? Stop being mean. Where is Dad? WHERE IS DAD?!" She screamed at her mother. Her mother flicked her cigarette into the yard, stood slowly and simply said, "He is not coming back Penny and neither one of us can change it."

Penelope kept screaming at her mother as she walked into the house and closed the door. She followed her mother into the house, screaming at her, all the while she knew deep down inside something terrible had happened. "Mama", she whimpered, "What happened to Dad?" She began to cry. "MAMA Pleeeease!"

Penelope wailed and collapsed on the floor. Peggy Sue walked over, knelt down and stroked Penelope's hair. "Your father was killed in a car accident Penny. I'm sorry." She stood, walked into her room and closed the door.

Peggy Sue never claimed the body. She couldn't face the trauma, nor did she have the emotional fortitude to put Penny back together. So, she left it in the hands of the state. She called the local Sheriff and asked if he would be kind enough to send a picture of the accident site and its location. He was very confused by her request but he was too busy to entrench himself in any more details, he had enough to worry about. Peggy Sue placed the picture and small piece of paper in her secret photo album and closed the book.

Chapter 8

Penny rocked backwards and sat down completely confused. She stared at the picture on the cross and then back at the wrinkled directions in her hand. She must be lost; this cannot be the right place. Suddenly she was back on her bicycle so many years ago as the loss of her father kicked the wind out of her once again. She tore the picture from the cross as a paralyzing thought crept from the dark recesses of her mind and the universe slapped her into coherency as the jagged pieces of a troublesome puzzle finally came together. From deep within her, the glue that had held her broken pieces together gave way and a deep inhuman groan began to rise. Penelope tilted her head back, let out an excruciating lament and fainted, clutching a faded picture of Abigail.

Chapter 9

Bobby Perkins wanted to be a cop for as long as he could remember. His grandfather had served in law enforcement for 40 years, his father was getting ready to retire with 30 years under his belt and Bobby had just reached the 10 year mark. He recalled watching his dad button up his uniform, strap on his Sam Browne, pull the brim of his hat down low and stick his finger in Bobby's chest and bark, "Stop in the name of the law little man!" tickling Bobby as he did it. He idolized his father; he was Superman and Bobby was going to be just like him.

Bobby let his mind wander to the day he told his father he would be following in his footsteps; Jerry Perkins got up, put on a pot of coffee and asked him to sit down. He waited quietly as the coffee finished brewing, he poured two large cups and sat down across from Bobby.

"Son", he said, "I have anticipated this day for some time. Your grandfather had a similar conversation with me when I told him just what you told me. The journey you are about to

embark on will cost you more than you know.
From your side of this chasm, you see an
adventurous life filled with Hollywood heroics,
breathtaking adventure, righteous causes and
justice served. What I'm about to tell you is by
no means an attempt to sway your decision; it is
merely a father being responsible to a son he
dearly loves and would like to protect for the
rest of his natural born life. But I raised you to
think for yourself and do the right thing. I had a
feeling you were going to make this decision
and to be honest, I hoped you might wake up
one day and see a different path. I joined the
force with the same enthusiasm you have right
now, ready to right every wrong, slay every
dragon and save every damsel in distress. It
didn't take long for me to realize justice can be
a fickle mistress and just because you wear the
blue, doesn't guarantee respect or appreciation.
Be prepared to lose sleep, lose friends, lose
patience, lose compassion and unfortunately,
your innocence. You will spend days and weeks
driving the same old roads, dealing with the
same felonious human driftwood and

deforesting the earth with piles and piles of mind-numbing paperwork. Much of what you do will become so routine you won't even remember doing it, this is not what worries me. It will be the moments that never leave you that concerns me. The images that scar your virtue, the evil that haunts your peace of mind and the malevolent horror that lurks in the hearts of men. Those are the moments that worry me, because it will change you son, it will change you forever."

His father leaned back, sighed heavily and continued. "I was new just like you, been on the force barely six months. I remember the day like it was yesterday. An absolutely beautiful Sunday afternoon, the sky was sapphire blue, not a cloud in sight. A light breeze that felt like angel wings drifted in the cruiser window and the day had been quiet and slow. I was listening to the Cubs game when the squawk came over the radio; '10-16 please respond'."

His father went into detail describing his thought process as he pulled down an idyllic street in a small town that dotted the landscape of every town across America. It was too nice a day for a domestic disturbance, probably just noisy neighbors arguing over a stray beer can or loud music. He arrived at the house, a two-story Victorian with fresh paint. The front porch was equipped with several well used rocking chairs, resting beneath the shade of an old oak tree that belonged in a Disney movie. He got out of the car and listened, not a sound except the birds singing in the trees. He walked up the porch steps, glanced at the old rockers and knocked on the screen door. "Sheriff's Department", he called routinely. A man's voice returned his announcement with a simple "Come in." He opened the door and let his eyes adjust before making entry. He quickly scanned the room; "Officer Perkins with the Sheriff's Department Sir, we had a call there was a disturbance?", it was more of a question than a statement. He was taking in the contents of the room as he announced his presence and noticed the man on the couch; medium build, mid to late 30's, calm. He was reading a magazine. He continued his visual sweep and at first glance saw an infant in a wind-up Graco baby swing. The man sat quietly, reading his magazine while a cup of steamy coffee cooled on the coffee table in front of him.

His Dad stopped momentarily as he drifted into a moment that would slice the frayed edge of his lucidity for as long as memory served him. Bobby remembered his father looking down at the floor at that moment, clearing his throat in order to keep an ocean of sorrow from bursting through a creaking wall of valor.

"I kept looking at the baby swing Son, something wasn't quite right. I asked the man if I could turn the light on and he said, 'Of course'. I reached for the switch at the front door and the brutality of that moment changed me forever. I stood frozen in time and sometimes Bobby, I'm still frozen in that same spot almost 20 years ago.

The man had smashed the baby against the wall in a moment of rage, crushing its tiny head into a bloody gray mess, rupturing every organ and splintering the tiny spine that would never give a piggyback ride to a child of their own. Blood and brain matter stained the wall as the lifeless baby swung back and forth. The man never looked up from his magazine. I told him not to move as I stepped onto the porch and radioed frantically for backup and an ambulance.

I never went back into the house Bobby. I seriously considered killing him. He was an emotionless monster, calmly reading a magazine and drinking coffee as he continued to turn the hand crank on this macabre tiny pendulum of death. I sat down on the steps, took my badge off and waited for backup. I knew if I went back in, I would have emptied my gun. That image has never left me Son and you are about to venture into a life that will take from you more than its capable of giving."

Bobby pulled off to the side of the road, the same spot he pulled up to ten years ago as the lessons from his father echoed into a crowded, sorrow lined memory. He grabbed the mic from his radio and replied in mindless staccato; "Unit 26, 10-23". Bobby got out of the car and saw a young girl lying on the edge of the road, directly in front of the cross, he knew too well. Before he could key his mic and call for an ambulance she suddenly sat up; she was completely unaware of his presence as he slipped up next to her, knelt down, placed his hand gently on her shoulder and very calmly said, "You must be Penny Lane."

Chapter 10

It was raining as the call came across; "Unit 26. Please respond 10-50". It was a routine call on his first night as a Deputy Sheriff. He responded and flipped the switch. His adrenaline raced as he imagined getting to the fender bender in the nick of time to calm a damsel in distress on this cold rainy night. He was there in minutes and rolled up on two smoldering hulks of twisted metal that had careened into the ditch. His fantasy extinguished as quickly as it had begun.

"Unit 26 10-23. 10-52, possible multiple injuries. Need assistance."

He jumped out of the car as his lights danced on the wet black road and gnarled metal like some bizarre carnival ride gone amok. His heart racing, he pulled his hat down low and began to make his way toward the carnage. The sound confused him at first; he stopped in his tracks and touched his revolver.

A gut wrenching, other world moan that sounded like some kind of animal, drifted in the rain. "What in God's name is that?" He thought. He stopped to listen, a little shaken and it came again, this time a wail. The hair on the back of his neck rose as goosebumps covered his entire body, "Oh my God that's a man!" He began to run toward the sound, he came around the wreckage and froze. A mountain of a man, covered in blood was kneeling next to the jagged remains, holding the lifeless body of a young girl.

His wail was bloodcurdling. Bobby stood dumbfounded as the man continued to try and pull her free while holding the child.

Time completely stopped; Bobby would recall later in his report that he could not remember how long he stood there. The man was completely oblivious to the officer's presence as Bobby finally knelt down within a few feet and, as calmly as he could, said help was on the way. The man never even acknowledged him.

"Sir, SIR!" he yelled. The man finally looked up and Bobby would never forget the mask of anguish that covered his face as he continued to scream, "NOOOOOOOO NOOOOOOOO"

Bobby stood up, feeling completely helpless as the rain dripped from the brim of his hat and that's when he heard the singing. He turned his head to listen and heard it again. He recognized the song and thought maybe the radio was still on in of these mangled wrecks. He walked around the sizzling hulks. The vehicle was resting on its roof so he got on all fours and shone his light into the front seat. The man looked to be medium build, there was a deep gash in his forehead and his neck looked twisted out of place. He was holding a wrinkled bloody picture in his hand as he sang words that Bobby recognized. "Penny Lane is in my ears and in my eyes", the man groaned as he gasped for another breath, "there beneath a blue suburban sky..." His voice trailed off as he rasped for air.

"Sir, Sir, help is on the way. You hang on buddy, ok?" Bobby pled.

The man managed to turn his shoulders so he could see the officer.

"Her name is Penny Lane", he twisted with a groan and handed Bobby the picture. "Tell her I love her." And with that he slipped away.

"Sir, HANG ON SIR! HANG ON! HELP IS ON THE WAY!" Bobby yelled to no avail.

He sat back on the wet pavement holding a picture of a little girl who was about to get the worst news of her life. From the other side of the knotted mess the wailing continued as the ambulance finally arrived, drowning out the inhuman cry of sorrow that Bobby Perkins would never forget.

Chapter 11

Penny looked up at the strange man in a brown uniform and saw the badge. Her head was still spinning as she stared at the man who had just called her 'Penny Lane'.

"What did you say?" she asked. "Who are you? How do you know my name?!" Her voice rose an octave. "Ma'am, its ok", Bobby spoke softly. "My name is Officer Bobby Perkins; I'm with the Sheriff's Department. Can you stand up?" Her gaze never left his face as she placed her hand in his and he helped her up. "Can we get out of this rain?" Bobby asked. "We can sit in the cruiser, if you like." Still Penelope's gaze never left his, "Yes, yes we can." She replied. They took a few short steps, Bobby opened the passenger door for her, helped her in and quickly got in the driver's seat. Bobby keyed the mic, "Unit 26 10-6".

He looked at Penny and she was still staring at him with a desperate look of intense question. She was still clutching the picture and he immediately remembered holding the picture of her. He could see the resemblance in her eyes; the little girl in the photo had grown up.

For a moment Bobby felt an intense rush of emotion as the voice of her father bounced off the walls of his memory and an incredible pang gripped his heart. He always felt like he had been given a mandate by a dying stranger. A promise he had never been able to fulfill. The man in the car had only one thing on his mind as he lay dying, and it was this girl sitting in his cruiser.

"Please tell me what is going on." It was more of a demand that a question. She was completely undone; she had come to say goodbye to her father and the universe had mocked her long anticipated moment of closure. She was teetering on the edge of a complete breakdown. Bobby finally broke his silence; "Miss Lane, I was the first officer on scene the night of the accident."

"You were here?!" Penny blurted out. "Was my dad alive? What happened? Why is Abigail's picture here? WHAT IS GOING ON?! HOW DO YOU KNOW MY NAME??" She screamed.

Bobby paused just enough to let her breathe and gather what little bit of composure she had left. She was shaking, Bobby turned the heat up.

"Penny...can I call you Penny?"

"Yes, of course", she snapped.

"Penny, I rolled up immediately after the accident occurred. I was a brand-new Sheriff's Deputy and this was my baptism." Bobby paused, "I heard your father singing."

Penny burst into tears and moaned so deeply it startled Bobby; as if a piece of her soul just left her body.

She gathered herself, stared off into another world where her father was still alive and said; "Let me guess, he was singing Penny Lane." It wasn't a question; it was a statement. A gossamer shadow of a smile touched the edge of her lips and disappeared just as quickly as fresh tears followed a trail that had seen far too many for a girl as young as she.

She sighed heavily, looked out into the rain and turned her head toward Bobby. Her eyes were red, swollen and as blue as the sky was not. Her emotion was spent.

"What did he say?" she asked

Chapter 12

Bobby never understood why no one came to claim the body nor ever inquired of the accident. He kept the picture Mr. Phillips had handed him that fateful night and for months after the accident he would wake in the night as Jack's voice echoed along the rainy streets of Chimera.

He had complied with the widow's request and sent her a picture of the mile marker.

Bobby took it upon himself to include the location and directions, he never knew why until now.

And now she was clenching those faded directions in her hand, along with the wrinkled photo she had torn from the cross.

"Officer, what did he say?" Penny asked through the tears that would not cease. "Please tell me. I miss him so much, I wish I had been in the car with him, at least we would be together."

Bobby had never felt so helpless in his life, he wanted to take her hand, wipe her tears and assure her that she was going to be ok, but he couldn't. He was a just a stranger in a brown uniform; a bit player in a bad afterschool special with no lines, no plot and not a single rehearsal. His ten years on the force felt like ten minutes as he grasped for something, anything to comfort this broken girl in a universe that decided to snatch the closest thing to heaven she had ever known.

"Penny, will you come to the station with me? I have something to show you", Bobby did not know what else to do. He had held on to the picture Jack had given him, tucked away in a small lockbox in his desk.

Penny sighed heavily, "I don't think I can drive." She leaned back in the seat, completely resigned and emotionally spent.
"Don't worry Miss Phillips", Bobby assured her, "I'll get your car to the station."

Bobby escorted her into an old brick building that had certainly seen better days. In its juvenescence it had housed several women working for the suffragette movement. A small plaque in the lobby gave tribute to their daring and determination. No one really cared anymore. The building had gone into disrepair until a local contactor remodeled it and rented it out to several attorneys and a title company. They closed it again, left for greener pastures and the County purchased the dilapidated structure for pennies on the dollar, gutted it and turned it into a weigh station for human driftwood and heroes.

Bobby walked Penny to his desk, grabbed a spare chair and had her sit down. He knelt down next to her and asked if she was ok. "No, I'm not Sir. Would you be? I'm soaking wet, I'm tired, I'm confused and I am angry." Penny just shook her head.
Bobby wished for the wisdom of Solomon but the only thing that came to mind was a fortune

cookie he read after the leftover Kung Pao he had for dinner.

"A wise man listens to his heart. A foolish man listens to cookies."

"Can I get you some coffee?" he asked.

"Please. I would love some." She looked up and smiled at Bobby for the first time. She was beautiful. She had to be at least ten years younger than him yet her eyes held an ageless sorrow mingled with a sparkling zest for life; a playful sun held captive by a grieving moon. Bobby had learned a long time ago to trust every instinct he had when it came to people. He wondered at times if he was just becoming cynical and hard? That was one of many things that worried him about this job.

"Cream and sugar?" he asked.

"Yes please. Thank you", she replied.

As he walked towards their shoddy breakroom, he knew instinctively she was ready to let go, that's why she had come this far.

She wanted to say goodbye.

Bobby watched her sip the scalding coffee as if it were a magical elixir. Her eyes closed as she warmed her hands on a chipped mug he found in the cupboard. She let the steam drift over her face as he sat quietly.

She finally looked up and stared at him.

Bobby cleared his throat and began. He held a small grey lockbox that looked like it had fallen out of the back of a moving truck. It was beat up but as durable as the memories it held.

He opened it and stared momentarily, not really sure how this was going to go, although he was pretty sure where.

He looked up at Penny and realized she was still holding the picture of Abigail.

Suddenly the question she had screamed at him earlier echoed in his memory. He wondered why he didn't remember it? He was trained for detail.

"How do you know her name?" he asked.

"What are you talking about?" Penny replied.

"The girl in the picture you're holding."

Penny looked down at the crumpled photo and without looking up she said, "It's Bud and Annie's daughter." As the words fell from her lips the realization crept like a dark shadow across her countenance and stole her breath. "Oh My God" was all she could say. She closed her eyes again and laid her head in her hands. Bobby let her alone for a minute before he asked her again, "How do you know them?" "How do you know Bud and Annie? Did your mother contact them?" Bobby realized he was interrogating her so he stopped and waited. Penny said nothing, she lifted her hand, began to rub her forehead and slowly shook her head back and forth to say no.

"Penny, how do you know them?" Bobby asked again.

"Bud fixed my car yesterday." Penny's voice was disconnected as if she were narrating a story she had just read. "I was on my way to find my dad. I found these directions in a photo album my mom had hid from me. I was so angry at her I just left and started to drive. I broke down outside of Quincy and a nice man named Bud towed my car and fixed it for free." Penny was crying again. "He took me to his house so I wouldn't have to stay in a motel and I met his wife, Annie. We had dinner. We laughed and we cried, she was very sweet, so kind", Penny whimpered, "and I felt so bad that she had lost her little girl. Sorrow had somehow found us in this stupid universe and connected us, but I had no idea how close until now."

"Bud killed my father." Penny said with a resigned sadness.

Chapter 13

"You did not know them?" It was more of a statement than a question. Before she could reply Bobby added, "so they have no idea who you are?"

Bobby furrowed his brow deeper than it was ever meant to go and asked a question that didn't get an answer; "What is going on?" His eyebrows raised as they looked up at each other, both afraid to speak.

Bobby took a breath and began; "I was a new officer that night Penny, as a matter of fact it was my first call, a car wreck, a fender bender. I was eager to get there; it was raining and I figured it was some damsel in distress, stuck in a ditch and I would be a hero and come to her rescue. I have never been more wrong; it was a scene from a movie set. The rain was coming straight down, the lights from my cruiser were bouncing off the twisted metal like an evil DJ at a dance party in hell. I immediately called for ambulances because I couldn't imagine anyone living through that carnage. I jumped out of the cruiser to see if I could help and that's when I heard Bud." Bobby stopped talking as the sound that had haunted him for so many years came back like a freight train. He closed his eyes tightly and focused on the task at hand.

"It sounded like a wounded animal Penny; it scared the hell out of me. I thought maybe they had hit something like a deer, maybe a bear, I didn't know. I put my hand on my pistol, the hair on the back of neck was standing straight up as I stepped around to the other side of what used to be a car." Bobby stopped again as his memory painted a vivid picture, he wished he could forget. "He was sitting on the pavement, there was blood all over him and he was holding Abigail." Bobby's voice caught in his throat as he fought back a tsunami of emotion. "He had managed to get Annie halfway out of the passenger window, I thought she was dead. I knew the little girl was gone and Bud wailed like I have never heard before in my life and I hope I never hear it again. It was inhuman, it

cut me to the quick Penny, I can still hear it."
Bobby's voice trailed off again. "I had no idea
what to do. I just stood there, helpless. I just
wanted to go home Penny. But I knew home
would never be the same."

Bobby cleared his throat as he regained his
composure.

"The rain stopped suddenly, it just quit. I
thought it was odd at the time but it was
certainly welcome. That's when I heard
someone singing." Penny was barely holding
onto her emotions as a single solitary tear, ran
down her face.

Bobby waited, not for effect but because he
wanted to weep with her, he wanted to hold
her, assure her that everything was going to be
ok, but he knew he couldn't.

Bobby began again. "I half expected a
paramedic to come walking around the
wreckage singing a Beatles song. It seemed so
surreal; I was drawn to it. I moved around to
the other vehicle; it was upside down so I knelt
down to take a look and there he was, singing
like it was just another day." Bobby furrowed

his brow. Penny watched every facial expression, taking in every detail, every nuance, every syllable.

"I got his attention and told him the ambulance would be there in minutes. I told him to hold on. I told him I loved that song. I told him I was a huge Beatles fan. I told him I would sing it with him." Penny watched Bobby's polished façade begin to crumble as the weight of that moment stole his breath and an army of tears broke rank and forced their way past his impenetrable defenses.

Penny waited as he gathered himself quickly.

"He didn't look at me Penny, he looked through me."

Bobby reached into the box as he was speaking. "He handed me a picture of you and him. It was the way he spoke that has never left me Penny. It was as if he were introducing us, but it came with an oath. He said; 'This is Penny Lane. Please tell her I love her'. And he closed his eyes."

Bobby handed the picture to Penny. She tried to smile but the agony was too much as the wrinkled old friend in her hand pulled her forward in her chair. Bobby caught her as she burst into tears. He held on as an ocean of sorrow poured out of her, one tear at a time. It was then Bobby realized he was crying just as hard.

Minutes passed like hours as their tears finally dried up. Bobby was a little embarrassed as Penny leaned back and asked for a Kleenex. He quickly got up, went to the restroom, splashed cold water on his face and brought her some tissue. She was holding the picture and smiling as he came back into the room. She never looked up.

"It was my 10th birthday. He was always on the road selling the latest and greatest invention but he always made it home to see me. Every other weekend and two weeks in the summer; my days were spent waiting for him. He would always pull into the driveway with Penny Lane blaring on his car stereo. I loved him so much. He had driven through the night to make it home for my birthday and he had a brand new bike stuffed in the back seat. I rode that bike the entire weekend and now I wish I had spent it with him. That was the last time I saw him. Two weeks later I was riding around the front yard waiting for him to pull up with the music blaring. I wanted him to see me on the bike. I was going to race him to the driveway and of course, he would have let me win. My mom came out and sat on the porch. She never sat on the porch. She had a big glass of wine and a cigarette. Funny the little things I remember about that day; she didn't have a wine glass; she had a green Tupperware cup. She just watched me ride as she finished her wine." Penny never looked up from the picture, as if she were reading from a memory from a script. "She drank that whole bottle as I waited for him to come. I can remember it like it was yesterday. I knew something was wrong, I could feel it in my bones. I remember praying on my bike; "where's my dad God?"

Penny stopped as a better memory pinged down the hallway of her remorse.

"I remember one weekend he had got a bunch of old cardboard boxes from a moving company and he had set up forts all over the house." Penny was smiling now, almost giddy. "He had taped a bunch of them together and made a rocket, a submarine, a ship and a racecar. We spent the whole weekend playing in those cardboard boxes. We ate our meals in them, pretending we were in a spaceship or on a deserted island. I will never forget those times." Penny cleared her throat as she returned to the memory that stole her youth.

"I watched her tip that glass to get the last drop. She flicked her cigarette into the yard and called me. 'Pitstop come here.' She called me Pitstop. I guess it was her way of mocking the things she could not give. I never understood why she did not like him; I think she blamed him for not repairing the life she had ruined.

I rode my bike up to the porch and I cannot begin to describe the foreboding I felt at that moment. I knew something terrible had happened.

She simply said, 'your father is not coming home this weekend Pitstop. Get used to it.' And she got up and walked into the house."

Penny kept staring at the picture, as if she were drawing some sort of resolve from it.

"I got off my bike and screamed at her. Where is my DAD?! I followed her into the house and ran in front of her and yelled again. Where is my DAD?! She shooed me away and told me to go out and play." Penny shook her head.

"I was certainly a persistent kid then; I wasn't going to let her off the hook that easy. I remember jumping on the couch so I could be at eye level with her and I screamed at her one more time; where is MY DAD?!

She leaned forward and got nose to nose with me and said, he is gone Penny and he is never coming back."

Penny sat quietly for a few minutes.

"That was the only time she has ever called me Penny. And I knew he was gone. I never knew how or why or what, I just knew. I still waited for him though, the weeks rolled by, and I would pack my Betty Boop backpack and wait for him to pull in the driveway with the music blaring, but he never came. Before I knew it, ten years have come and gone and I am here with you."

Penny's eyes never left the photo.

"I never got to say goodbye and that is why I came Bobby. I found your directions and I came to get some closure, to find some peace; I came to talk with him one more time. I came to tell him I love him. I came to say goodbye.

I had a feeling he had left me something. I knew he would never leave without telling me why. I knew he wouldn't."

Penny finally looked up from the picture. She looked deeply at Bobby, the same way her dad had looked at him the night of the accident. Bobby felt his heart roll up like a window shade.

Penny smiled, with tears in her eyes and said, "Thank you for waiting for me. My dad knew you would."

Penny looked down at the picture again, a lithe smile touched the corners of her face as she kissed her fingers and touched them to her father's face. She whispered "I miss you Dad" and laid her hand over the picture.

Chapter 14

Bobby waited and let her stay in the moment. He had seen a lot of bizarre things in his ten years on the force but this one certainly took the cake. Four hours ago, he was wondering if he would get lunch and where he was going to eat it.

Now, he was a small piece in an incredible puzzle the universe just dumped at his feet. Bobby wondered if maybe, he might find an answer to some of his own questions.

Bobby finally broke the silence. "Bud did not kill your father, Penny." Bobby was deliberate but tender. Before he could go on Penny replied; "What do you mean? Are you saying it was my dad's fault?" Before Bobby could answer she began to escalate; "Please don't tell me my dad killed Abigail! Oh my God." Bobby stopped her quickly; "Penny no. Your father killed no one. Look at me. Penny look at me please." Penny looked at him, barely holding back the well of sorrow that seemed to have no bottom.

"It wasn't your dad's fault and it wasn't Bud's fault. There was a witness that came forward a few weeks later. There was another car, they had just passed the semi when it fishtailed. They knew there were other cars behind it but they kept going and hoped everyone was ok. A week later they saw the accident in the paper and called the police. We don't know which car hit which car and at this point it doesn't matter, because it wasn't their fault. Wrong place at the wrong time Penny. I know that doesn't help but I have no answers for the ocean of questions each day brings."

"Why does Bud think he killed Abigail?" Penny stated in a halting staccato. "He thinks he killed my DAD. He doesn't know the other car was my dad? This is unbelievable irony or some twisted form of poetic justice. The universe SUCKS!" Penny looked up angry, shaking her head back and forth. "How in God's name did I end up in their house?" It wasn't a question Bobby could answer so he didn't try.

"I slept in their house, I sat at their table. I fell in love with them." Penny raised her hands. "We laughed together, we cried, she even held me. I felt so bad she had lost her daughter. We were kindred spirits that night and I have never felt so close to anyone. She made me feel safe, she gave me hope. Bobby, I pulled out of their driveway this morning wishing she was my mom. This can't be real."

Bobby didn't know what to say but he felt like he needed to say something. "Whatever delivered you into the hands of Bud and Annie, almost ten years to the day, from the same accident that claimed your father is bigger than both of us. I don't have answers for how or why, only what. And the what is you; you're all collateral damage to an accident that took pieces of your life, pieces of your heart and a piece of your soul. I know that doesn't help but that is the What".

Bobby continued as delicately as he could. "The three of you are broken pieces and you all keep

cutting your fingers trying to put yourselves
back together again.
This is a puzzle I cannot put together, maybe
that's why you're here. Maybe you're the
missing piece Penny."

Bobby paused, took a breath and continued.

"I went to Abigail's funeral."

Bobby stopped, not for effect but because the
grief he had locked up for so long, threatened
to break down the careworn splintered door
that held it back. He was tired.

"There was a lot of people there that day, it was
easy to go unnoticed. They had a lot of friends
and a lot family. I stood far in the back and
watched."
Bobby looked Penny in the eye and said; "I was
looking for you. I went because I thought that
maybe you and your mom might be there.
I don't know why I thought that, maybe just
naivety. I had the picture of you and your dad in

my pocket. I wanted to give it to you. I kept looking through the crowd for the little girl in the picture. I wanted to find you, kneel down in front of you and hand you the photo. I wanted to tell you what he said and tell you the song he was singing. I wanted to tell you everything was going to be okay. I wanted to tell you to be brave and that he would always be with you. I wanted to tell you he didn't suffer."

Penny sat spellbound.

"I visited Annie in the hospital too. I felt like I was supposed to. I went a few times. Bud was a brooding mess; he was pretty banged up; his bruises would heal but his heart wouldn't. He sat in a chair next to Annie and never left her side unless he ran to the cafeteria or the bathroom. She was so kind; she kept thanking me for saving her. I told her, Ma'am your husband saved you, I was just doing my job. She would shush me and say, 'You saved us both' and then she would take my hand and say thank you. I saw Bud in the cafeteria on one of those

visits and tried to buy him a cup of coffee. I have never seen a more broken human being. I worried about him. At the time I really thought he might try to take his life. He thanked me for the coffee. He didn't remember me and I didn't think it was a good idea to remind him. That was the last time I went to visit them. I have seen them a few times at the accident site; they come four or five times a year. They always hang a fresh picture and leave flowers. I have gotten a few calls on the radio about a stranded vehicle and a woman in a wheelchair and I know who it is. I have always wanted to stop and say hello again. I don't know if they would remember me and I don't know if they would want too.
I wouldn't."

Bobby sighed heavily and noticed his dirty shoes.

It was late in the day and the sun was setting. Exhaustion came like a freight train, stealing their resolve and leaving both of them numb and hungry.

"Penny, do you want to get something to eat?

"Pleeeease!" Penny stretched the word for emphasis. "I want to eat everything on the menu and sleep for a week."

"Okay, get your coat. I'll drive."

Chapter 15

They sat in the corner booth of a diner that time
had simply ignored. The floor was a black and
white checker board. The counter was lined
with red stools and red booths that hugged the
walls. It looked like a theme diner except it was
not, it was just old.

Penny wolfed down a double cheese burger and
helped herself to some of Bobby's fries when he
went to the restroom. Bobby ordered coffee
and Penny sipped on her tea as the awkward
silence kept them from making eye contact.
Bobby finally broke the silence.

"Penny can I ask you something?"

"I think you just did." Penny replied playfully,
the food had energized her for the moment.

"Funny girl when you've got some food in your
belly." Bobby smiled.

"Sure, ask away. I can't imagine this day getting
any more bizarre." Penny halfheartedly smiled.

"Well, I don't know any other way to ask this so
I will just ask; Penny why didn't your mother
come and get him?" Bobby was visibly shaken.

"I waited but she never came and I have never been able to shake that night. Sometimes it feels like something I watched on TV a long time ago and today, it feels like yesterday." Bobby looked down at his coffee cup and softly shook his head. "And before you answer I might as well get this other little nugget of weirdness off my chest"

Before he could say a word, Penny cut in; "Sure Officer, and please be very selective because this day just hasn't been crazy enough." Bobby looked up and Penny was grinning.

"Ok." It was more of an announcement than a question. "I own the entire Beatles collection.........On Vinyl!" Bobby stared at her, waiting for a reaction.

Penny looked at him without changing her expression, then slowly lowered her head, spotting a cold fry she had overlooked. She began to play with it.

She was still shaking her head slowly as she spoke. With a whispered resolve, as if she were preparing to deliver the worst news anyone could hear, she simply said;

"I have the entire Norman Greenbaum collection on cassette." She said mockingly; as if they were two old fishermen swapping tall tales.

Penny finally looked up and flicked the French fry at Bobby. It hit him right in the badge.

Bobby looked down at his badge and slowly looked up at Penny.

"Ma'am, that could be considered assault with a greasy weapon. But I could possibly overlook the offense if you will simply answer this one question. Who the hell is Norman Greenbaum?"

Penny played along as a southern belle; "Why Officer, how could you possibly not know the esteemed Mr. Greenbaum? He stole every young girl's heart in the Tupelo Baptist Church in 1969. Spirit in the Sky may have been his one and only hit, but as far as the lil angels at TBC are concerned, that's all Mr. Greenbaum needed".

Penny batted her eyes and fanned her face with a laminated placemat.

Bobby laughed and flicked the French fry back across the table, hitting the placemat she was holding.

"Police brutality"; Penny said in a playful southern voice.

They looked at each other and laughed.

"Do you really have that guy's collection on cassette tape?"

"Yep. The whole entire collection."

"Wow, I didn't know he had a collection."

"Oh, he does," Penny said as a matter of fact. "And I have it. All ten songs, surprisingly, fit comfortably on one cassette. I got it at a garage sale with my dad, it cost me a dime. We took it back to his house and tore the garage apart looking for his old cassette player. We listened to it the whole weekend. He told me to hang onto it, it might be worth some money one day."

Penny trailed off, "That was the last time I saw him."

Penny got serious, "My mom did not come and get him because she is broken. And I cannot fix her. No one can."

"Love and hate cannot inhabit the same space for very long Bobby, it's impossible. It creates a venomous sludge that leeches into the bloodstream of civility and chokes the hope once laid; a deadly poison that slowly kills the host.

My Dad was a lover and a dreamer, my mother a vindictive wounded soul that held forgiveness hostage until it starved. This is my inheritance, Bobby. Twenty years old and I feel like an old woman at a crossroads; a place that takes most people a lifetime to find, if they bother looking at all. You would think it's an easy choice but I have no map; only a moral compass that is bent and spinning like a top in a hurricane. My dad used to say the most dangerous are the last to fall. I sure don't feel very dangerous Bobby, but I'm still standing."

Penny paused and took a breath. "My mom told me he was in a bad car wreck but that's all she ever told me. She said we would never see him again and that was that. Up until a few days ago, that's all I knew. Until I found her old photo album and set out to find him".

Penny looked at Bobby as if to gauge his resolve and then began a chilling narrative;

"She is asleep on the floor in a hallway outside a locked door, in a strange house. She thinks her mother is in there; she is 5 years old.
She has cried until there are no more tears to cry, exhaustion has taken the place of terror and she has finally succumbed to a fitful, dreamless sleep.
Hundreds of miles away a young father languishes in absolute brokenness, as helpless

as the child he adores, lies quivering on a stranger's floor.

He pleads with a God whose heavens are brass this night, as the jagged shadows of a lonely motel begin to squeeze his soul and fray the edge of his lucidity.

One pebble in a glassy sea of remorse, sends ripples of regret across the lives and years of the unexpected; on a cold morning, in the middle of nowhere."

"That's how I grew up Bobby."

"The first few times were horrifying. After a while I got used to being left somewhere; in a hallway, a spare room, with a stranger, until she finished her tryst and decided to pack me and her remorse in an overnight bag and head back to the life she hated. I learned not to ask questions or complain. She would stay in bed for days after, and I was left to myself. I learned to survive and I leaned on my dad. He knew what was going on, he wanted me to come and stay with him but my mom would have nothing

to do with it. I was the weapon she used to cut
him. He tried to reason with her, over and over
but she wouldn't listen; she just yelled and
screamed. She would call him a loser and laugh.
He was getting what he deserved.

I'm not sure where I would be if not for him. He
taught me imagination; he taught me to look
for solace in every storm and find the flower in
the junkyard." Penny smiled as a memory
danced in her imagination. "We actually went
to a junkyard once on one of our adventures.
He liked finding old things and restoring them.
He would weave some magical tale about the
previous owners and their journey as he held an
ordinary piece of junk in his hand."

Penny giggled.

"And one time, he actually found a lily in a
junkyard. A beautiful flower that stood so
proud. It was such a contrast; I will never forget
it. He called me over and said I could touch it
but "Do Not" pick it. It had defied the odds and
grew where there were no other. He told me it
was a testament to determination and all things

beautiful, and like the flower, we should bloom where we are planted.

He knelt down, looked me in the eye and said; Penny, 'beat the odds baby. Bloom and be beautiful wherever you are'. And he kissed me on the cheek and we went home with an old washtub.

I have always wished things were different, but they're not. So, I choose to be different. I choose to beat the odds and be beautiful. For Jack Phillips, my beautiful dad."

Penny leaned back as one last tear found its way down her cheek. She stared faraway, into a tomorrow that seemed a lifetime away.

Chapter 16

It was late, the day seemed like it had lasted forever as a wave of melancholy crashed over both of them.

Bobby broke the silence.

"Penny we both need to get some rest. I have an idea, but it will have to wait until tomorrow."

"That's fine Bobby, it's not like I have a packed schedule at the moment. Can you drop me at a motel?" Penny asked.

"You don't have to stay in a motel Penny. I have a spare bedroom; you are more than welcome to stay at my place. It isn't much but it's home." Penny smiled. "I'd like that, Bobby. Thank you."

Bobby pulled into a one car garage that was crowded with good intentions. An unhung pegboard rested against the wall along with half a dozen two by fours. A five-gallon bucket of paint, a few sheets of drywall and shelf unit that was still in the box, lined both sides of the garage. Bobby made sure he left room for her to get out as he squeezed his torso between the unfinished plans and his car door.

It was small but surprisingly homey. Bobby had pictures of his parents, nieces, nephews and his graduation picture from the academy. A few antiques littered the front room, some forgettable furniture, a stack of books and a record collection that was displayed proudly next to a turntable that reminded her of her dad. The kitchen was small but functional, it certainly didn't look like Bobby was aspiring to be a weekend chef. A loaf of bread had been spun in the bag and laid down with the whip tucked underneath; a typical man maneuver. The dish drainer had one plate, a cereal bowl and a handful of silverware that would probably never see the cabinet and drawer they came from. An old cast iron skillet rested on the back burner, waiting for someone to bring home the bacon. A coffee pot took center stage on the counter and looked like it got more use than anything else in the kitchen. A small, lonely breakfast table rested under the only window in the galley kitchen and had become a catch all for magazines, keys, and mail.

Bobby led her down a hallway that looked like a hotel innkeeper had decorated it. A small end table hugged one wall with an old lamp that looked like it belonged in a garage sale. Several pictures lined the walls with one in particular that stood out. Penny stopped to take a closer look and Bobby stepped up behind her. Two men in uniform and a little boy stood in front of an old black and white police car that looked like a prop from the Andy Griffith show. The boy stood between the men wearing an oversized police hat and a smile that stretched from ear to ear.

It was Bobby.

"That was 20 years ago Penny, I was ten. My grandpa finally retired from the Police Department after chasing bad guys, bad jokes and bad puns for 45 years. He spent his entire life cruising the streets of a little bitty town. He turned down every promotion, he liked being around town. Working high school football games, taking inebriated kids home to disappointed but grateful parents and having coffee with the locals every Saturday morning at the diner. He retired on his 65th birthday and didn't know what to do with himself. He tried to find a hobby but all he knew was police work. Wasn't long after he just gave up. We buried him a few years later." Bobby shook his head.

"I've been doing this for ten years and somedays it feels like forty-five. I wonder if I'm really cut out for this kind of work Penny." Bobby's voice trailed off as he stared into yesterday, wondering if it might be a harbinger of things to come.

Penny turned and looked at him and felt a pang for this man she had just met. He was still in uniform, and it was at that moment she realized she had been in the same clothes for two days.

Suddenly she was exhausted.
"Bobby, would you mind if I took a shower?"
"Of course not."

He moved to the bathroom quickly, as if to check to make sure it was presentable. He came out with a handful of towels and told her to make herself at home.

Penny took a long hot shower and washed away a day that felt like a lifetime. Bobby had left fresh towels, a robe and offered to throw her clothes in the wash. She obliged.
He led her to a very plain guest bedroom complete with a Futon, a small dresser, a night stand and a picture of a mountain range that looked like anything you might find in a doctor's waiting room. Penny didn't care, she just wanted to sleep and hope tomorrow would take her one day farther away from today.

Chapter 17

Penny woke to the luxurious smell of bacon and coffee. She wanted to sleep until tomorrow but she knew she needed to put a bow on this macabre adventure. She sat up and noticed her clothes on the chair. Bobby had washed and folded them for her.

Penny smiled.

She dressed quickly, ran a hairbrush through her hair and tiptoed down the hallway into the kitchen. Bobby was hovering over the stove watching eggs cook when she peeked around the corner.

"Good morning, Officer." Penny said playfully. "Do you moonlight as a short-order grill cook?"

Bobby handed her a steamy cup of coffee and a crispy piece of bacon and replied, "You tell me." Penny closed her eyes, sipped the hot ambrosia and demolished the piece of bacon in three bites.

"Well, if the law enforcement thing doesn't work out for you the world could always use another cup of coffee and a plate of bacon."

Bobby had replaced the clutter on his small breakfast table with two sunflower placemats, a pitcher of orange juice and a small stack of buttered toast.

"Penelope Phillips, table for two." Bobby said in the worst English accent Penny had ever heard. She started laughing as she walked over to the table and waited for him to pull her chair out.

"Ok Garcon, the only way you can redeem yourself from that hideous accent is to come over here and pull my chair out for me."

Bobby happily obliged.

They both sat and made small talk over eggs, bacon, toast and coffee.

Penny put her fork down and looked at Bobby, "I really appreciate your kindness, Bobby. I didn't know there were still guys out there like you. Thank you for breakfast, thank you for doing my laundry, thank you for everything.

And speaking of thanks," Penny paused, "Do you know where my car is?"

Bobby smiled. "It's in my driveway."

Penny arched her eyebrow, "In your driveway? Did you sleep last night or have you been running around cleaning up after my circus monkeys?"

Bobby laughed, "Yes I slept, I had it towed to the station and one of the guys drove it over last night. You can be on your way if you like or…" Bobby paused.

"Or what?" Penny asked.

"Or, you can take a little ride with me."

"And where would you be taking me Officer?" Penny replied playfully.
Bobby hesitated and Penny picked up on his uncertainty.

"What's on your mind Bobby?" Penny had a way of cutting to the chase, she was a survivor and Bobby admired her grit.

"I spoke with Annie this morning. I told her I needed to come and see her today." Bobby paused again and looked intently at her, "I would like you to come with me."

Penny didn't flinch; "Does she know I am with you?"

"No, I told her I was bringing a friend she might like to meet."

Penny leaned forward, "I don't know if I'm ready for this Bobby. My God, can I take a breath or do I have to figure this all out in a few days? This is all so bizarre."
Penny got up and refilled her cup. She sat back down, sighed and stared out the little window over the breakfast table.
She sighed heavily, looked Bobby in the eye and said;

"Yes. Yes, I will. If I don't do this now I never will. I have to go home eventually and I can only imagine how that little reunion is going to go so….let's go. I need to get this done."

Penny sat her cup down and asked, "Why did you call her?"

Bobby cleared his throat.

Chapter 18

Annie filled Bud's thermos with fresh coffee and reminded him to be sure he came home for lunch; they were having company.

Bud asked who it was, but Annie stayed tight lipped, it was a surprise.

He told her he might be tied up with a job, but she insisted and Bud knew he would be there even if the President's limo blew a tire in front of his shop.

Bud mumbled as he walked out the door, he was feeling a little melancholy and had been thinking about Miss Penny Lane. She had been gone one day and he was busy wracking his brain, wondering if he had checked everything that could go wrong.

Annie wheeled her chair around as Bud walked out the door and she glided into the kitchen in anticipation of having company. She was very curious why Bobby would call and ask if he could bring a friend. He had stopped by a few times over the years, only when he was in the area. He even stopped up at the crash site in his patrol car once, shortly after the accident. She had not heard from him in over a year and found this meeting somewhat unusual. She shrugged off her feeling and stared into the refrigerator, looking for lunch.

Bobby looked off into space as if he was looking for a script that would not come.
"I don't know, to be honest. I've spent less than two days with you but I feel like I've known you my whole life. I was the last one to see your dad alive and something happened to me that night Penny. Somedays it feels like ten years ago and today it feels like it was just ten minutes ago. It probably sounds weird but I have never been able to shake it. I've been to dozens of accidents and a laundry list of horrendous crimes and none of them have affected me the way that night did. Please don't take this the wrong way or think I would ever diminish your loss or your grief, but it changed me and I can't figure it out."
Bobby stared into his empty cup and cleared his throat.

"I've been waiting for you. I know that sounds so crazy but I knew you would come. I carried that picture of you and your dad around for several years and would make a point to drive by the crash site every couple of weeks. That's how I ran into Bud and Annie. I never told them anything about your dad or the picture he gave me, they were so broken, I was afraid to show them a picture of the little girl who lived, waiting for a father who did not."

Bobby got choked up and took a moment.

Penny was wiping her eyes with a napkin.

"I have to help Penny, and I don't know what that means." Bobby was desperate.

"If I never do anything else in this life, I have to see this through, I can't keep cutting my fingers on the jagged edges of this unfinished memory."

One lone tear broke rank and ran down Bobby's face. It took all his willpower to abate the river of sorrow that lay behind a failing rampart.

Penny never looked away as she reached out and laid her hand on top of Bobby's.

He looked down at her tender fingers; a thousand tears had splashed into this ivory cup that lay gently upon his calloused hand.

Bobby closed his eyes as the warmth from her hand pierced the thin veneer that imbued his guarded heart. For an instant he did not feel alone anymore, he wanted to break down but he knew he could not. His career had left him a lonely young cop with the wisdom of an angry sage and the cynicism of a jilted neophyte. He felt like loose change falling from a hole in his pocket and all he had left were pennies.

He looked up; afraid she would move but she didn't. She was still looking at him; a gaze that took more than his breath. She was innocence wrapped in jade; a paradox of all things good and all things gone awry, yet there was a flicker of hope; a flame that Bobby wanted to sit next to on a cold night and warm his weary soul.

They sat motionless for what seemed like hours. Penny smiled, patted his hand and said, "Let's go Bobby."

Annie pulled Bud's favorite casserole out of the oven and set it atop of the stove. It was her version of Shepherd's Pie and one of Bud's favorites, although there was not much Bud didn't like. A thick mixture of ground beef and sausage, mashed potatoes, peas, carrots, cheddar cheese and a layer of potato chips on top. Annie moved around the kitchen like a figure skater; a relish tray appeared, place mats, a pitcher of iced tea and a tray of oatmeal raisin cookies.

She wiped her hands on a dishtowel as she heard Bud's truck pull into the drive.

She turned her chair with practiced ease as Bud walked in the front door.

"Hello Beautiful." He tipped his head back and sniffed the air. "Ok, now you have my attention and my curiosity; who are we having lunch with?"

"Bobby."

A shadow crossed Bud's face as his good mood passed quickly, he wished the President's tire had blown in front of his shop now. "What's the special occasion?"

"He didn't say, he asked if he could bring a friend over. I imagine it's a special lady he would like us to meet. I think it's sweet Bud."

"Maybe so," Bud replied. "We haven't heard from him in a while. She must be something special for him to bring her here. He's always liked you Annie, but then again you have that effect on most people. Especially me." Bud smiled and let his apprehension pass.
"This might be fun," he thought.

Bud was washing his hands when he heard the doorbell ring. He hollered from the kitchen as he haphazardly hung the dishtowel over the oven handle; "Officer Perkins you better have a warrant or a bucket of chicken if you wanna get in this house!" Bud turned the corner and froze in his tracks. Annie, who normally a picture of grace, sat motionless with a puzzled look on her face.

"Miss Penelope!" Bud stammered as his knees buckled. "Oh my God, did something happen to your car?! Are you ok? I knew I should have taken another look at it. Where is it? I'll go get it and take care of everything. I am so sorry..." Annie cut him off immediately.

"Bobby and Penny?!" It came out more like a question than a hello. "My goodness this is a surprise, I had no idea you two knew each other."

Penny knelt down and grabbed Annie's hand, "Up until yesterday we didn't Annie. He found me sitting by the side of the road at the Payson exit." Penny handed Annie the picture of her and her dad. Annie lifted her hand quickly to her mouth, failing to silence the gasp that escaped her lips.

"Oh my God," was all she could say. Annie was completely undone as Bud moved to her side still unaware of what was happening. He knelt down, while glaring at his lunch guests as Annie handed him the picture. Bud looked at it, looked up at Penny and asked, "What does this mean? Annie, what's going on?" Bud looked up at Bobby and Penny, "Why are you here?"

Annie grabbed Buds hand; "Bud, this is Jack Phillips' daughter."

"Wha..? Jack who?" Before the question could completely slip from his lips the realization began to sink in as he stood up slowly; his face twisted in utter confusion as he slowly shook his head back and forth. Bud held onto Annie's chair, to keep from falling, as limbic lag slammed into him like a freight train.
Bobby moved quickly and steered Bud toward the couch before he collapsed. Penny stood completely still as the crushing weight of sorrow engulfed the room.
She did not want this to happen.

Bobby moved through the room swiftly and efficiently; almost like he was working another accident. He moved Annie next to Bud, slipped his arm around Penny and moved her toward the chair next to the couch.

No one spoke for several minutes.

They sat in the roar of deafening silence, waiting for words that would not come.

Chapter 19

Bobby stood on the periphery of a broken landscape and forced himself to become an officer in order to navigate the emotional carnage before him. As he cleared his throat to speak, Penny looked up at him with a clarity that silenced every concern and alarm that was clanging in his head.

She looked at him exactly the way Jack did the night of the accident.

Bobby's mouth gaped open as she walked over and softly touched his face like a gossamer wing.

"Thank you, my friend," her words were a song; a melody that had traveled for over ten years and had not lost any resonance. Bobby closed his eyes hard as the tears he had locked away for so long found a path of least resistance and slid gracefully down his cheeks.

His quest was complete.

"My father thanks you too Bobby."

Penny walked over to Bud and knelt down in front of him.

"Mr. Bud", she said so softly it was almost inaudible, but Bud heard her.

"We don't have to be broken anymore. Fate may have bound us by tragedy but we have a choice today to heal. Mr. Bud, I've been broken a long time and I'm tired of being broken. My dad was my whole world; he was all the family I had and somehow, he managed to bring me to you and Miss Annie. Of all the tow truck drivers in the world, you picked me up that day. I was so freaked out at first but I know better now. It was my dad; he had a way of bringing people together with a song, a story, a corny joke or his wild imagination." Penny smiled and shook her head.

"Sure, I miss him, but I have a feeling he must have spun a few whoppers in Heaven to pull this off."

Penny looked around the room and took a moment to look at the three of them with a palpable warmth and gratitude.

She grabbed Annie's hand and kissed it. "We lost so much that night and we can never get it back. But you know what I think Annie? I'm pretty sure my dad is playing "Fort" with Abigail right now and they have the most amazing fort in Heaven."

Bobby couldn't figure out if Bud and Annie were crying or laughing. Penny moved around them like an angel, pouring grace and balm over their weary souls. She was elegance and mercy personified; a picture of all things beautiful.

He was completely smitten and undone.

Annie turned toward Bud, "Please pick me up."

"Are you sure?" Bud asked with concern

"Yes Bud, please pick me up and hold me up."

Bud stood in front of her chair, locked the wheels and ever so gently lifted her out of the chair. He held her as if she weighed no more than a feather.

"Now turn me around dear so I can face Penny."

Bud maneuvered her so she was facing Penny and held her with a secure grip.
Annie looked Penny in the eye and spoke in a tone that no instrument would ever play better, "Please come and let me hold you."

Penny slipped into her arms as if she had been waiting her whole life.

Bud held onto Annie as she held onto Penny, and they wept.

"Let me go Bud, I need to stand."

"Are you sure" Bud replied.

"Yes, I need to do this."

Bud began to loosen his grip as Penny tightened hers until she was holding Annie up by herself. They stood together for as long as Penny could hold on. She leaned forward and gently placed Annie back in her chair. Annie never let go of Penny's hand nor did she shift her gaze. She waited for Penny to look up and then she spoke; "Penny, I know we just met but I believe you are an answer to a very old prayer. Our lives have been knit together for longer than I can remember and I want you to know that as long as Bud and I have breath, you have a place to call home. Abigail's room will always be your room. I am weary of the past Penny and although I don't know what the future holds, I don't care, as long as I can hold you."

Penny laid her head in Annie's lap and whispered "Thank you."

Epilogue

So many things have changed since I first sat down to write the story of Penny Lane; the table has been replaced, more than a few years have passed and my life has changed for the better. I wasn't sure how her story would end or where she would land to be honest. She certainly had her share of opportunities and hardships along the way but she overcame and managed to become an enigma of grace and benevolence wrapped in charity. She inherited more than just whimsy from her father, she captured his devotion, his tenacity and an incredible ability to see tomorrow long before the day is through. Although this story looks like it's finished, I know hers is just beginning……..

And it looks like I've got to go, my girls are home.

"Daddy! Are you coloring?"

"Eleanor Rigby, where have you been?"

"We went to the grocery store silly, to get supper. And my name is ELLIE!"

Bobby leaned down to give his daughter a bear hug. "You are sooo beautiful little lady."

"Can I play one of your records Daddy? Please? I'll be careful just like you showed me."

"Sure SugarPop, but only if you play your mama's song."

"Yes!" Ellie sprang from his grasp and raced into the living room.

"Well, hey Shakespeare, are you still working on that story of yours?" She walked in with her hands full of plastic grocery bags.

"Hey baby." Bobby turned the last page of his journal, put his pen down and closed the book. "I think it's done Penny Lane. How are you?"

"I'm good handsome, can you give me a hand with supper? Bud and Annie are coming for dinner tonight."

"I can't think of anything I would rather do."

Bobby grabbed a few bags from Penny's overloaded arms, kissed her cheek and set them on the counter.
Ellie squealed from the other room as she turned up the music, "Grandpa BUD is coming!!

Penny opened the blinds as the sun burst through the window and her favorite song came on.

Bobby slipped up behind her, spun her around and began singing along. Ellie squeezed in between them as they twirled and sang at the top of their lungs,

"Little darling, it's been a long cold lonely winter. Here comes the sun, Doo-n-doo doo, here comes the sun and I say it's all right." [2]

♫

References

[1] McCartney, P., & Lennon, J. (1967, February 13). *Penny Lane* [Vinyl]. George Martin.

[2] Harrison, G. (1969, September 26). *Here Comes The Sun* [Vinyl]. George Martin.

Rick lives in Southside Virginia with the love of his life, Janet.

BIG MOUTH PUBLISHING

Kaiser Enterprises

©2020

"May time be a gentleman who tips his hat,
looking away as you pass."
Rick Kaiser